PARIS

FROM THE AIR

Translated from the French by Elizabeth AYRE

PARIS FROM THE AIR • PHOTOGRAPHS BY YANN ARTHUS-BERTRAND • TEXT BY ANNE ARTHUS-BERTRAND • CHÊNE

From high in the sky, the eye of the camera zooms in on the horizon. Everyone pores over the pages, trying to pinpoint a familiar neighbourhood, a well-travelled street, or even a window looked out of each day. The camera captures the smallest detail, enters clandestine corridors, offers a behind-the-scenes glimpse of the city. It is a secret door to private Paris. These magical aerial photographs give new meaning to the romantic lighting over the city's rooftops heralded by poets one hundred times over, and the backlight of the rising and setting sun gives familiar landmarks a surprisingly – at times startlingly – new appearance. The view embraces the city, yet peers incisively into all dimensions, from the more grandiose sides to the more intimate, anecdotal ones. It is a vision which, until now, only lovers have been able to conjure up in the wildest of their dreams. Smiles of complicity will break out among Parisians who recognise the neighbourhood where they grew up or first fell in love. One amusing discovery follows the next, from hidden balconies to rooftop swimming pools ...

What first hit the eye are the magnificent perspectives envisioned by those who shaped the city. It's as if the architects and artists designed Paris to be viewed from the sky. What better approach could a photographer dream of for shooting exceptional sites like the Louvre, les Invalides or Place de la Concorde? The only way to capture unique photographs such as these is by helicopter. The camera boldly targets its prey, defying "natural" obstacles, then takes some distance to plan the next strategic foray. It hovers over sealed portals, nose-dives into courtyards, and slips into secluded gardens, then leaves detail behind to take a vast panoramic shot stretching from the Tuileries Gardens to the Arc de Triomphe. Paris is stripped naked.

There is nothing more satisfying than poking fun at the pigeons or conscientious tourists. Breathe the air, explore your senses of taste and touch, and the secrets of the city which everyone dreams of are in the palm of your hand. Paris is a living, vibrating, joyous city which responds in kind to the love you hold for it in your heart.

A bird's eye view reveals how each quarter of the city represents a slice of history. The architecture, road system, shops and social structure of each area is unique. But Paris has been subjected to so many various forces, both constructive and destructive, that it is difficult at times to recognise the stamp of each master beneath the successive layers of make-up.

Follow the Seine, the river which nourishes the heart of the capital with eternally new blood. Listen to the fervent beating of the heart of France. Paris has seen and lived through so much joy and sorrow that the stones themselves are engraved with the passion and hatred.

Over two thousand years have elapsed since a tribe of ancient Gaul, the Parisii, settled on the island of Lutetia. Today, crowds of businessmen, students, tourists and gawkers cross paths in every direction. The city capriciously wrapped its coils around its island core, reaching from the Gallo-Roman city wall to the fortifications of Thiers, ever eager to conquer new territory. Portals were erected and bridges laid out, with palaces, churches and monuments solidifying this breathtaking expansion. Men toiled for long periods of time, sometimes their whole lives, to complete these buildings. Whether simple villagers or outstanding citizens, scores of Parisians fought to make the tiny boat of the Lutetia water merchants – the symbol of the city's emblem – into a great fortified ship. Its motto: "Fluctuat nec mergitur", or "It floats, but never sinks."

Lutetia, as Paris was once called, was occupied by the Romans for over five hundred years. Baths, arenas and other vestiges of the Roman occupation reveal that Paris's Left Bank was an area of burgeoning growth as early as the first few centuries A.D. Few traces of the great Merovingian constructions on the Left Bank remain today. During the Carolingian era, Paris was neglected, then

weakened, as a result of the Norman invasions. A timid awakening marked the beginning of the Romanesque period. The Saint-Germain-des-Prés church, built between 990 and 1014, is the forefather of all Christian monuments in Paris.

Gothic art first made its appearance after the founding of the Capetian dynasty in the beginning of the 12th century, namely in the churches of Saint-Martin-des-Champs and Saint-Pierre-de-Montmartre. The style reached its peak with the construction of Notre-Dame cathedral on Ile de la Cité, in the heart of Paris. Long centuries of relentless battles took place here as this temple of faith vied for power with the temple of law, embodied by the nearby Capetian palace. The omnipotence of the clergy was strengthened in every domain by political turmoil, endless wars and widespread ignorance. Nothing but churches and theological schools were built.

At the same time, Kings were striving to bolster their power, both inside and outside the capital. Philippe-Auguste shielded his capital with a thick crenellated wall and sought protection inside an impregnable fortress, the Louvre.

With nearly 130,000 inhabitants squeezed into 350 streets, Paris was somewhat cramped within its early walls. Its infamous narrow streets were unhealthy, and the more affluent inhabitants sought refuge outside the city wall. The city developed simultaneously on both banks, unprecedented in the history of urban development. The north was the centre of commerce, the south – dubbed the Latin Quarter – was the hub of intellectual activity.

The 14th century produced an extraordinary man, Etienne Marcel, a political leader who was provost of the merchants. In an effort to bolster municipal authority vis à vis the absolute rule of the monarchy, he commissioned the Hôtel de Ville (the City Hall), to be built on the Place de Grève and ordered a new wall to be constructed on the Right Bank. The latter was completed by Charles V when he protected the Saint-Antoine portal by building the famous Bastille fortress.

Paris was so ravaged by civil wars at the time that architecture was designed more to meet the need for protection than for shelter. Even the castle at Vincennes, called the Versailles of the Middle Ages, was designed as a fortress... in the countryside. After a hiatus due to the Hundred Years' War, a rash of construction projects commissioned by the clergy marked a return to peace and piety. Gothic art became increasingly flamboyant from the 15th century on, the Saint-Nicolas-des-Champs church and the mansions of the archbishop of Sens and the Cluny abbots being the finest examples.

After deciding in 1527 to settle in Ile-de-France, François Ier introduced the Renaissance style which he had discovered in Italy. Under the aegis of the architects Pierre Lescot and Jean Goujon, the reconstruction of the Louvre resulted in an architectural entity of incomparable beauty. Catherine de Médicis and, in turn, Henri IV worked to link the Louvre to the Tuileries palace via the Grande Galerie du Bord-de-l'Eau. Secular architecture also developed during the Renaissance with the construction of the Collège de France, the Hôtel de Ville and the Place des Vosges.

In a dramatic departure from custom, the Pont Neuf was the first bridge built without houses on it. It quickly became a favourite spot for Parisians to meet, with the lovely Place Dauphine stretching towards Ile de la Cité.

Paris underwent many transformations during Louis XIII's reign as the Right Bank developed. The centre of the city, which moved towards the Louvre, was flanked by two aristocratic quarters, the Marais on the east and Saint-Honoré – Saint-Roch on the west. The former became a highly fashionable area under Henri IV: gentlemen and noted members of the bourgeoisie set the tone for the entire city as they built superb mansions like those of the Saint-Honoré area, squeezing out vegetable gardens and orchards in the process.

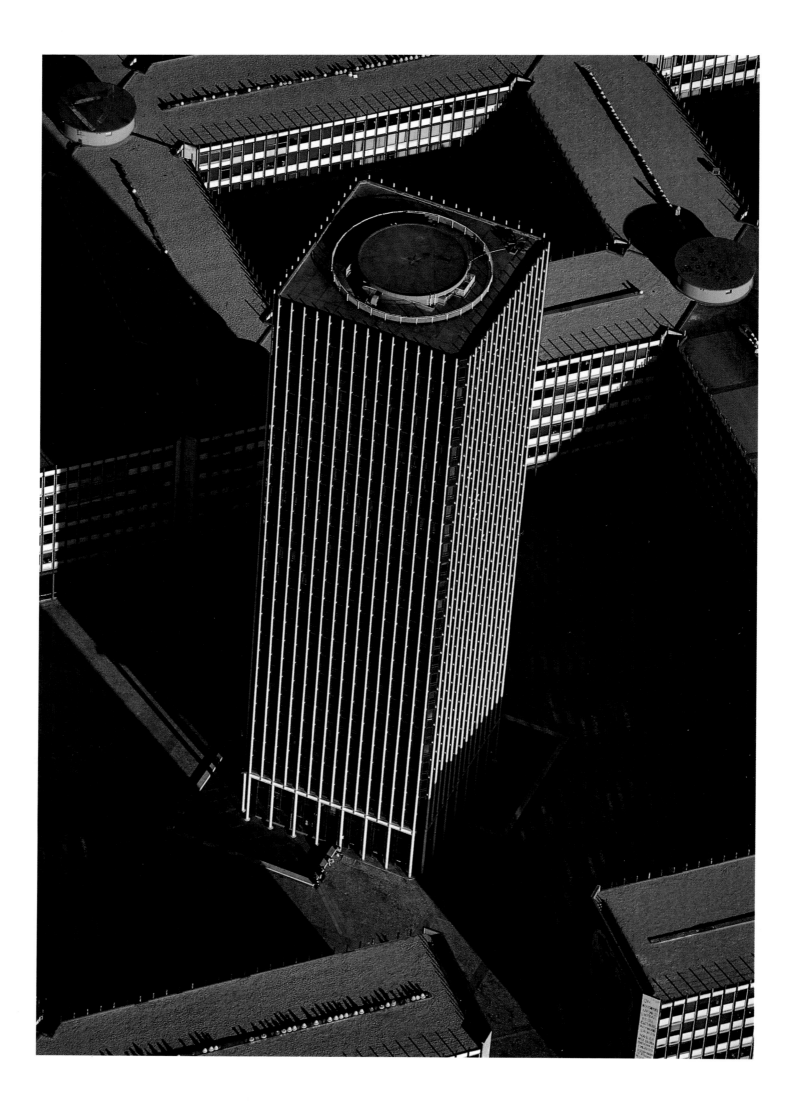

Acting in accordance with Richelieu's desire to extend his palace, the future Palais-Royal, Louis XIII expanded the walls of Paris. Sumptuous mansions sprang up in Ile Saint-Louis and in the area near the Louvre. Marie de Médicis, who had become Regent, commissioned Salomon de Brosse to draw up plans for her Luxembourg Palace. Guy de la Brosse founded the Jardin des Plantes, also located on the Left Bank, which was growing rapidly at the time. A great religious resurgence resulted in the edification of several churches. Saint-Sulpice, the Sainte-Marie temple and Val-de-Grâce all date from this period, which was still under heavy Italian influence.

Louis XIV may have preferred Versailles, but he didn't neglect the architecture of Paris, which flourished under his reign. A new Louvre was born: Le Vau quadrupled the size of the Cour Carrée, while Perrault erected his famous colonnade opposite the Saint-Germain-l'Auxerrois church. The glory of Louis XIV's rule was expressed through colossal public undertakings (the Observatory, the Institut de France, the Hôtel des Invalides and the Saltpétrière hospital), as well as in large-scale urban projects which determined the capital's new look. The architect André Le Nôtre laid out the promenade along the Champs-Élysées, across from the Tuileries. Ramparts on the Right Bank gave way to broad tree-lined boulevards. Jean Hardouin-Mansart designed two royal squares, the Place des Victoires and the future Place Vendôme. Louis XIV devoted the final years of his reign to religious art, however, namely to the Dôme church, which was the second church to be built at Les Invalides and a stroke of genius in terms of French classicism.

Under the Regency, large-scale projects were financed by private enterprise instead of receiving support from the King or the church. Reflecting a change in lifestyle, Parisian mansions were broken down into main buildings with courts and gardens. The Marais, which had become less popular in comparison to the trendy Saint-Germain-des-Prés quarter, still had its Soubise and Rohan mansions, however.

Newly developed areas were filled with dwellings which were as beautiful as those in the Faubourg Saint-Honoré, where the Evreux mansion was located.

Shortly after 1750, there was a resurgence of grand-scale projects. A fifth royal square was added, where the Place de la Concorde now stands. The École Militaire, the Panthéon and the reconstructed Palais-Royal heralded the age of classical nobility, which flourished under Louis XVI. The Hôtel de la Monnaie, the Saint-Philippe-du-Roule church, the Odéon theatre and the Pont de la Concorde are some of the finest examples. Designed in a neoclassical style by Nicolas Ledoux, the portals of the Farmer-generals' wall, which served as customs gate-houses, were striking in their magnificence. There was a flurry of private construction projects. The Prince of Condé expanded the Palais-Bourbon, and members of the nobility built a number of luxurious mansions.

When the furor of the Revolution had subsided, the Empire undertook huge construction projects, following the monumental tradition of the *ancien régime*. The grandiose perspective of the rue de Rivoli; the second gallery linking the Louvre and the Tuileries palace; the Arc de Triomphe at Étoile; the facade of the Palais-Bourbon (the French Parliament, and the Bourse (the Stock Exchange were erected to glorify the great emperor.

The Restoration continued to further the Empire's undertakings and re-erected royal statues torn down during the Revolution. The July monarchy bestowed upon the city eclectic neoclassical

monuments – the Luxor obelisk, the Colonne de Juillet at Bastille, and the ornamental facade of the Panthéon, for example. Louis-Adolphe Thiers, the King's Prime Minister, ordered the construction of a fortified wall flanked on the exterior by a series of separate forts. These proved very useful in 1870 during the Franco-Prussian war. The next wall of Paris was made up of the outlying districts, known as *le périphérique* (the beltway).

During the Second Empire, Paris expanded even further as it became more modern. Napoléon III commissioned the Alsatian town planner Baron Haussmann to redesign the capital in such a way as to create great sweeping perspectives, which were both prestigious and... reassuring.

In doing away with barricades, Paris became more majestic, but at the expense of its beauty. The area which best illustrates this philosophy of laying out broad boulevards linking important squares is at the Opéra, where the famous theatre was built as a culminating point of the sweeping perspectives. The Second Empire also saw a rise in the use of metal for various projects, notably for Pierre-Louis Baltard's market (Les Halles); Jakob Hittorff's train station (Gare du Nord); France's national library, (the Bibliothèque Nationale) and the Sainte-Geneviève library by Labrouste. The Eiffel Tower, built for the 1889 Paris World Exhibition, marked the zenith of this style.

Private dwellings of exceptional elegance were peppered throughout the more beautiful quarters, notably along the Monceau plain and the Champs-Élysées. At the same time, Haussmann focused on open grassy areas to breathe some freshness into the city. He redesigned the Monceau and Buttes-Chaumont parks, as well as the woods around Boulogne and Vincennes.

The Third Republic marked its entry with the reconstruction of buildings, such as the Hôtel de Ville, which were burnt down during the Paris Commune, an attempt by the citizens to take power in 1871. The Palais du Trocadéro was conceived for the 1878 World Exhibition; the Sacré-Cœur also dates from this period. A series of buildings serving a wide variety of functions – meeting halls, department stores, banks, theatres, stations, schools and hospitals – went up throughout the city. The invention of the elevator permitted construction workers to reach even greater heights.

The 20th century can be divided into three periods: pre-war, when Art Nouveau or modern style prevailed; between the wars or the era of reinforced concrete; and post-war, with its fixation on verticalism.

Hector Guimard and Lavirotte's Art Nouveau architectural style was particularly prevalent within the private domain. But there were also the World Exhibitions. The Petit Palais, the Grand Palais and the Gare d'Orsay, which were built for the 1900 exhibition, conceal audacious metallic structures beneath their pompous stone facades in a striking lack of innovation.

The uncertainty of the period between the wars was reflected in the city's architecture. Perret, Le Corbusier, Sauvage, Mallet-Stevens and others sought to create a "modern" ethic by relying on new materials like concrete; others limited themselves strictly to complete reproductions of classicism. The Palais de Chaillot and Palais de Tokyo, built for the 1937 World Exhibition, are illustrations of the latter.

The second half of the 20th century was marked by such vigorous economic and demographic growth that Paris was forced to extend its walls. The capital became a department in and of itself, surrounded by two suburban zones. Municipal authorities made an effort to modernise construction and improve transportation facilities. There was a vast wave of reconstruction projects which followed innovative conceptions backed not only by architects and urban experts, but also by administrative authorities and politicians. The Charter of Athens, with Le Corbusier being the most famous supporter, was proof of the degree of faith in technical progress. It was a question of keeping the city in stride with a modern world while preserving the capital's history and artistry – neither a simple nor risk-free task.

The urban development plan which was put into effect for Paris during the Sixties targeted nearly a third of the city for demolition and renovation. Traditional urban districts underwent radical changes; this included Maine-Montparnasse, the Seine waterfront, and La Défense, as well as the 13th, 14th, 19th and 20th districts (arrondissements). Two hundred and thirty thousand housing units were built between 1954 and 1975!

The *boulevard périphérique* (the beltway), on the outskirts of Paris, and the Georges Pompidou expressway on the Right Bank date from this time. Monuments such as the UNESCO building, the Maison de la Radio, the Science Faculty at Jussieu, the Palais des Congrès at Porte Maillot, the Communist Party headquarters on the Place du Colonel Fabien, the Montparnasse Tower and station, and the new Parc des Princes stadium are all proof of sheer economic and technological prowess.

At the same time, historical monuments and buildings were being renovated, as was necessary with the passage of time. Through the efforts of André Malraux, Paris regained its gown of purity. Named Culture Minister in 1959, he promulgated laws to protect historical landmarks from public or private depradation.

During the Seventies, attention was focused more on the suburbs than on Paris. A regional council for the department of Ile-de-France was set up in 1976. Investment in Paris-based projects diminished; emphasis was placed on quality, not quantity. Pressure by "conservatives" to preserve Paris's traditional appearance played a key role in the abandonment or suspension of certain projects. Plans for the multicoloured Georges Pompidou Centre of Art and Culture, better known as Beaubourg, sparked a great deal of controversy. The centre was completed, however, and inaugurated by President Valéry Giscard d'Estaing in 1977. New directives on developmental policy in Paris were issued that year: maintain the diversity of capital and services, while preserving the national heritage and historical sites. After centuries of being under state control, Paris elected a mayor in 1977. Jacques Chirac, who still currently holds the post, has taken a great interest in the city, devoting a good deal of time and energy to it.

During the Eighties, a series of large-scale projects were designed to create residential neighbourhoods, particularly in areas which were once hubs of activity. These were generally located in the outlying regions of Paris: Bercy-Tolbiac in the southeast; the outskirts of the basin at La Villette in the northeast; or the old Citroen factories in the southwest.

But it was the completion of several public works projects which marked this era. The Forum des Halles shopping centre and the Plateau Beaubourg, the conversion of the former Gare d'Orsay train station into a museum, the creation of a science and technology museum at la Villette, the Arab World Institute along the quai Saint-Bernard, and an Omnisports arena at Bercy were projects launched during Valéry Giscard d'Estaing's term and completed under the rule of his successor, President François Mitterrand.

President Mitterrand has launched many ambitious projects, such as the new Finance Ministry at Bercy, the Grand Louvre's pyramid of glass, the Grande Arche at La Défense, the Bastille opera and the Bibliothèque de France, Perrault's controversial library on Quai de la gare which is currently undergoing construction. Every project has generated its own share of controversy with respect to the presidents' architectural choices. But fortunately, Paris remains a hub of architectural innovation. Respect for the city is a high priority, yet modernisation is an imperative. Ambitious cultural projects and principal urban operations are generated in response to the intense international rivalry among sprawling metropolises. In a newly unified Europe, Paris must remain a modern, innovative city, given her role as the symbol of France.

PLACE DE LA BASTILLE

page 18
MAISON DE RADIO-FRANCE
Built between 1952 and 1963 by the architect Henry Bernard, the "Maison de la Radio" is a classic example of architecture which is both aesthetic and utilitarian. A film for television depicting a Kafkaesque universe was shot on location here.

page 19
THE SEINE WATERFRONT
A waterfront development project was launched during the Sixties to renovate the area in the fifteenth arrondissement where old chemical factories stood. The fifteen residential towers pictured here were designed by the architects Lopez, Pottier and Proux.

page 20-21
THE SEINE BETWEEN THE GRENELLE AND BIR-HAKEIM BRIDGES
The string of beautifully classic buildings along the avenue President Kennedy was broken when a rounded structure was built. The RER network, a kind of supersonic metro which speeds from suburb to suburb, cuts across the Seine to get to the quai de Grenelle.

page 26
THE NATIONAL ASSEMBLY (FRENCH PARLIAMENT), HÔTEL DE LASSAY AND THE FOREIGN AFFAIRS MINISTRY
Under Napoléon, the look of the Palais Bourbon, where the Foreign Affairs Ministry is located, was radically altered with the addition of an antique facade. The 18th-century Hôtel de Lassay is where the president of the National Assembly resides, while the 19th-century Quai d'Orsay is the seat of French diplomacy.

page 27
GARE D'ORSAY
Built in 1900 by the Compagnie des chemins de fer d'Orléans, the Gare d'Orsay train station fell into disuse as early as 1939. This huge iron and stone basilica, designed by the architect Laloux, was converted into a 19th-century museum designed by the Italian architect Gae Aulenti in 1986.

page 28-29
PONT-NEUF AND PLACE DAUPHINE ON ILE DE LA CITÉ
The graceful arches of the Pont-Neuf bridge meet at the tip of the Ile de la Cité, between the Place Dauphine and the Square du Vert-Galant. Inaugurated in 1607 by Henri IV, the Place Dauphine was intended as a spot for bankers and merchants to negotiate deals; it was close to the

Palais de Justice. The square, composed of thirty-two houses originally in white stone and brick, opened onto the facade of the Palais de Justice from 1874 on.

page 34-35
NOTRE-DAME CATHEDRAL
Anatole France described the cathedral as being "as heavy as an elephant, yet as slender as an insect". Conceived in 1163 by Maurice de Sully, bishop of Paris, Notre-Dame was completed a century and a half later. This masterpiece of Gothic art, nicknamed the parish of French history, was magnificently restored under Louis-Philippe's reign by Lassus and Viollet-le-

Duc. Its arches have been witness to public prayer and major national ceremonies.

page 36
ILE DE LA CITÉ
The Ile de la Cité is like a great ship, its moorings thrown up onto the banks of the Seine. The Square du Vert-Galant is the ship's bow, the Ile-de-France and Jean XXIII Squares are the stern. The steeple of Notre-Dame serves as the watchtower.

page 37
ILE SAINT-LOUIS
In 1858, Champfleury wrote: "There are a certain number of Parisians in Paris who have never been to Ile Saint-Louis and who, if they ever set foot there, would return even more astonished than if they had been to a small town in Provence." Today it is still a small village thriving on its own, with life heavily centred around the church.

page 22-23
THE SEINE BETWEEN THE CHAMPS-DE-MARS PLAIN AND THE CHAILLOT HILL
The two long arms of the Palais de Chaillot spread their 435-yard wingspan over the gardens and the great basin of the Seine waterfront. Built for the 1937 World Exhibition by the architects Carlu, Boileau and Azéma, this neoclassical palace houses a theatre and museum.

page 24-25
THE EIFFEL TOWER
AND THE CHAMPS-DE-MARS
The most famous monument in Paris was built between 1887 and 1889 by a gifted engineer nicknamed "the iron magician". At the inauguration of his tower, Gustave Eiffel climbed the 1,710 steps, brandished a huge French flag and exclaimed: "This is the only flag in the world which has a 985-foot pole!" Surrounded by beautiful French gardens, the Eiffel Tower acts as a lighthouse, both literally and figuratively. It originally served as a meteorology antennae, then as a radio and television antennae.

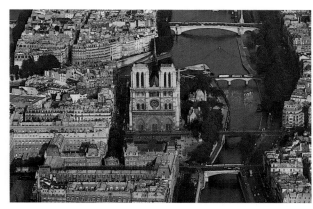

page 30
SQUARE DU VERT-GALANT
Two lovely Louis XIII dwellings stand at the passage leading to the Place Dauphine across from the Square du Vert-Galant.

THE COURT OF COMMERCE
Built by Bailly between 1860 and 1865, the elegant dome of the Court of Commerce towers over the charming flower market on the quai de la Corse.

page 31
SAINTE-CHAPELLE
PALAIS DE JUSTICE
Over the centuries, the Palais de Justice courthouse has engulfed the small adjoining streets to form a large block of buildings surrounding the Sainte-Chapelle church, village-like. Built in the beginning of the 13th century, the church was a monumental shrine conceived by saint Louis.

page 32-33
THE PARVIS AT NOTRE-DAME
The square in front of Notre-Dame is surrounded by Paris police headquarters (opposite the cathedral) and the Hôtel-Dieu hospital. The latter, which has no connection to its 12th-century predecessor, was built at the end of the 19th century by the architect Diet.

page 38
THE ARSENAL QUARTER
The Arsenal basin and its charming harbour occupy what was once a part of the old moat surrounding the Bastille. The basin links the Canal Saint-Martin with the Seine at the inlet at the Place de la Bastille.

page 39
THE NEW QUARTER AT BERCY
The elegance of the Omnisports arena at Bercy, designed and built by the architects Andrault and Parat, seems to be underscored by the long bridge-like design of the new Economics, Finance and Budget Ministry, built by Huidobro and Chemetov.

page 40-41
PORTE DE BERCY
This gateway to Paris, running along Charenton-le-Pont, is as grand as the entrance to any American metropolis. The overhead bridges spread their wings over clusters of railway sidings to better encompass the silvery roof of a gigantic shopping centre.

MAISON DE RADIO-FRANCE

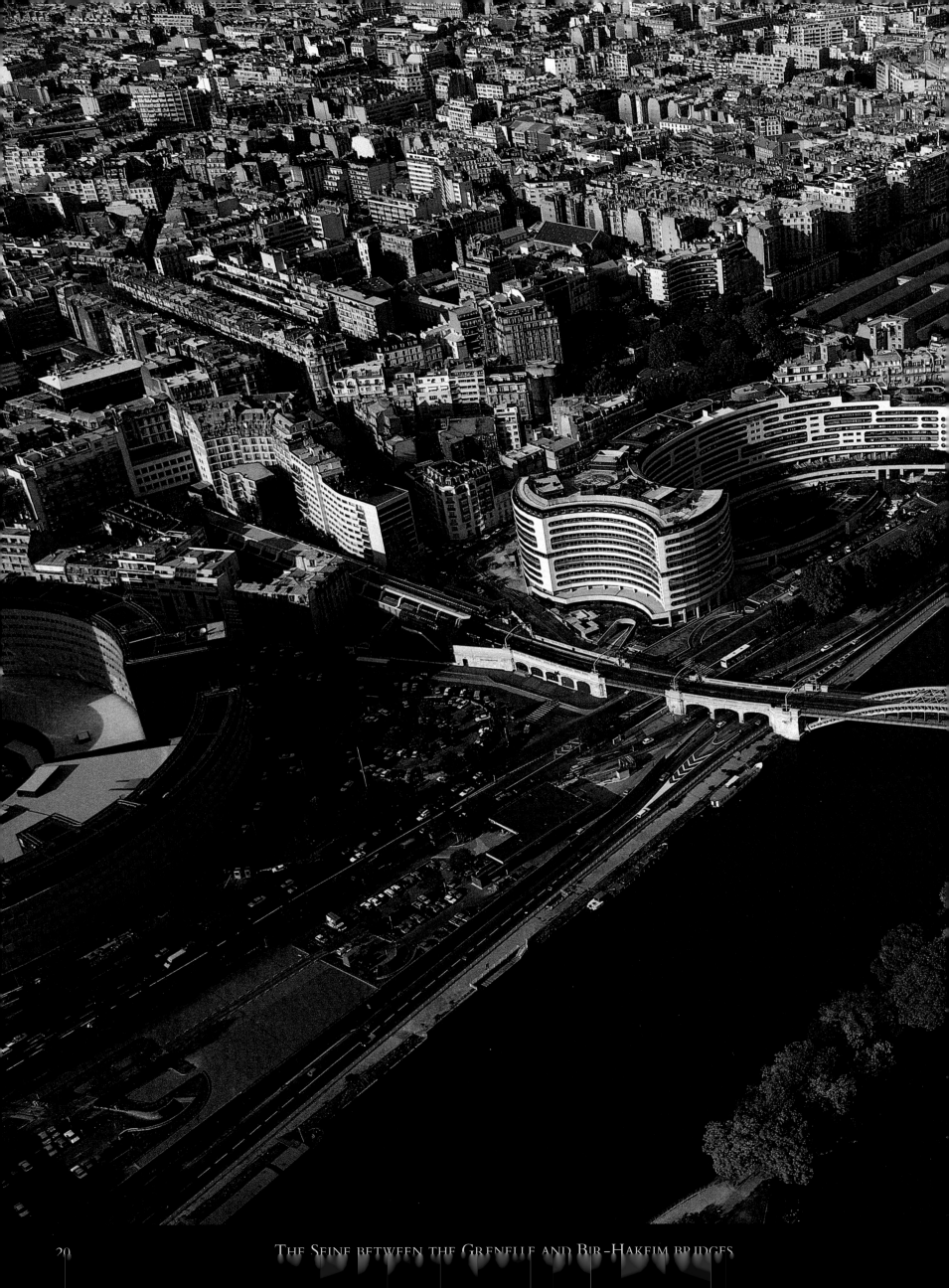

THE SEINE BETWEEN THE GRENELLE AND BIR-HAKEIM BRIDGES

THE NATIONAL ASSEMBLY, HOTEL DE LASSAY AND FOREIGN AFFAIRS MINISTRY

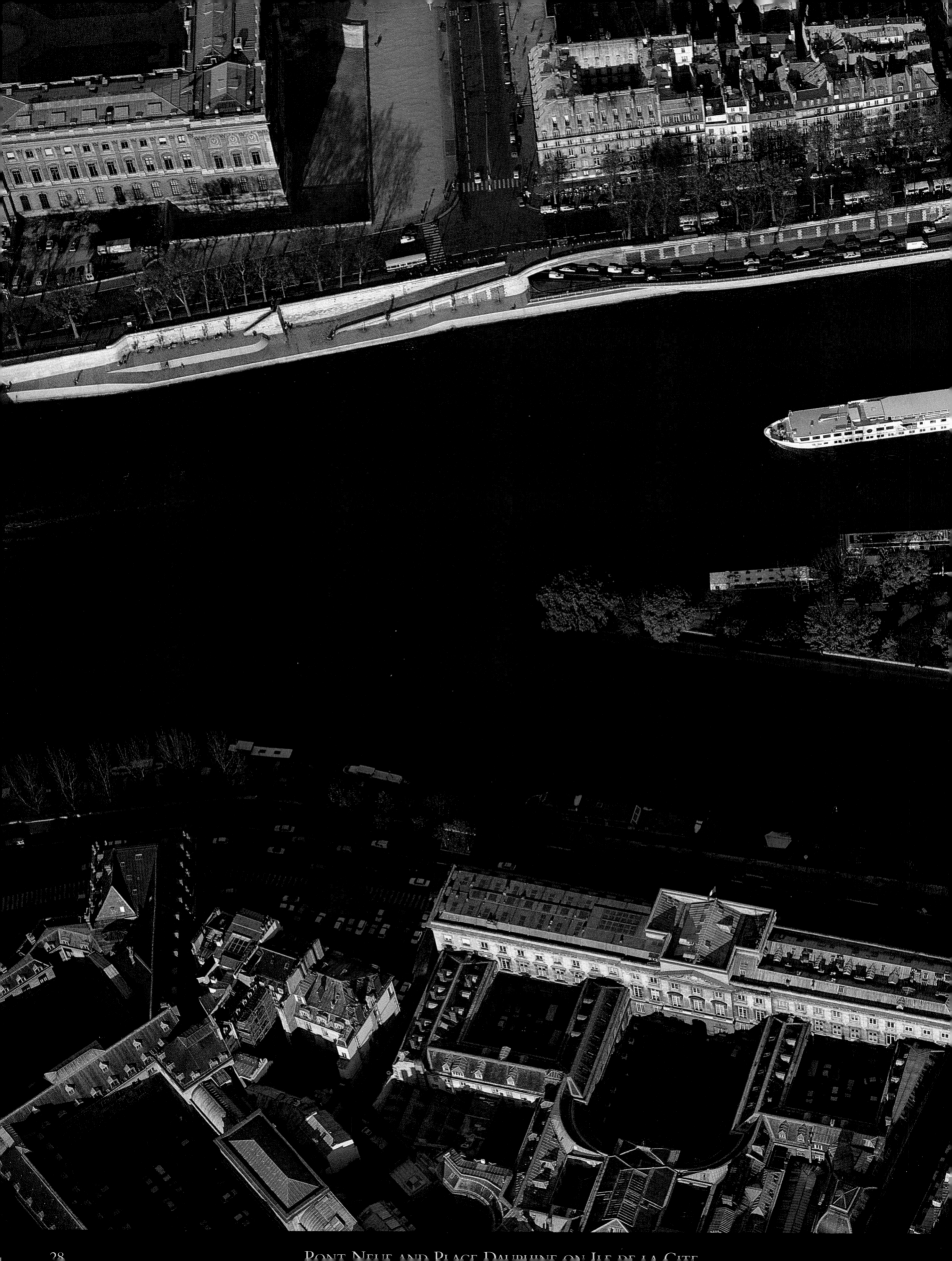

PONT NEUF AND PLACE DAUPHINE ON ILE DE LA CITÉ

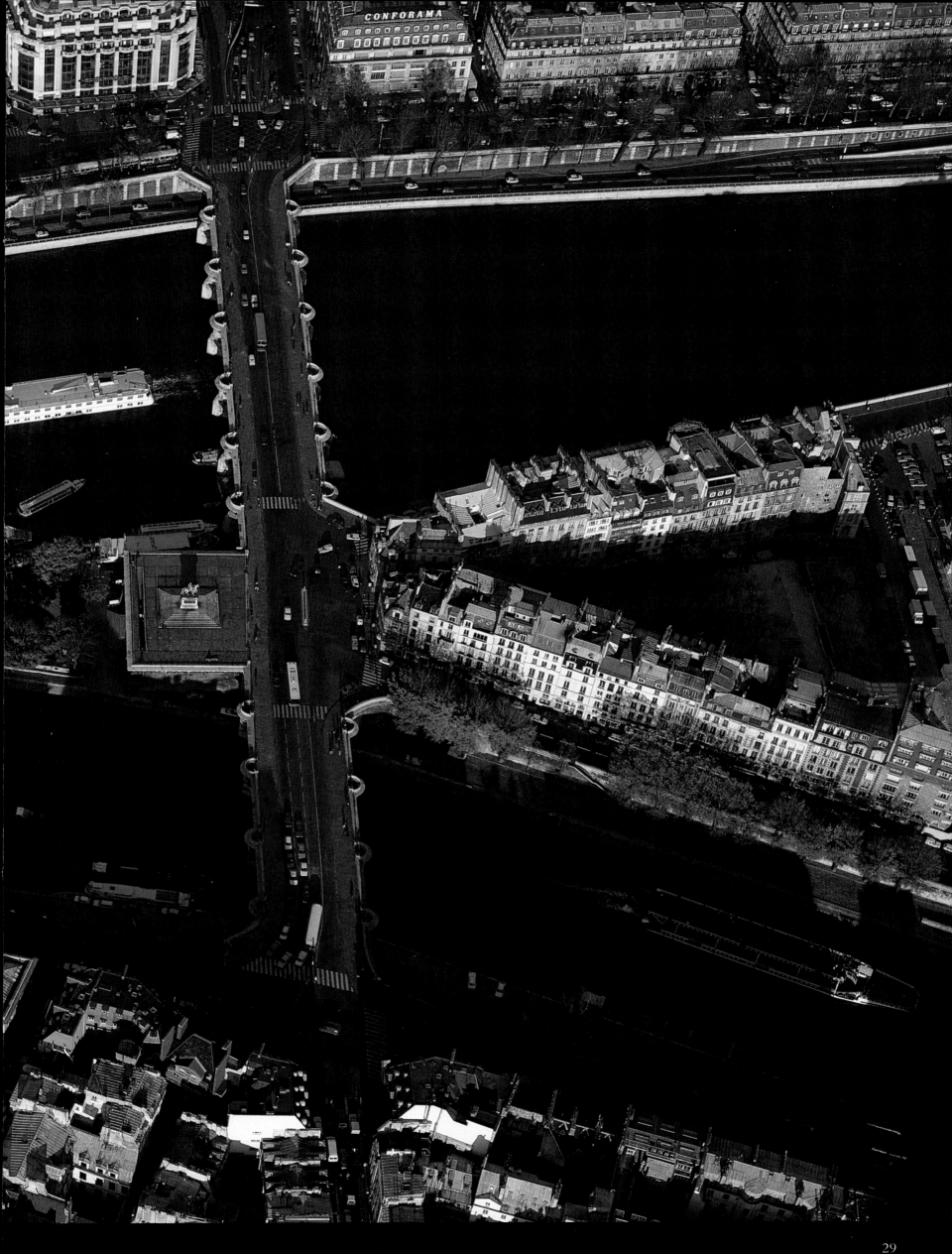

SQUARE DU VERT-GALANT   THE COURT OF COMMERCE ON ILE DE LA CITE

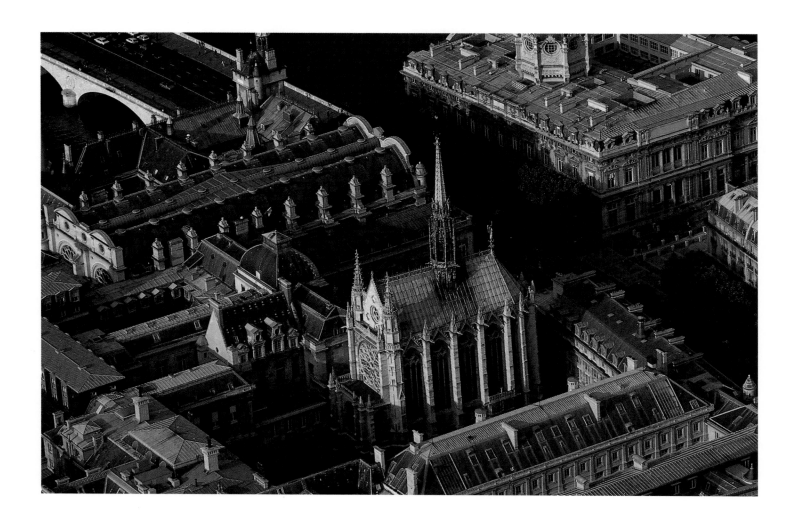

SAINTE-CHAPELLE ON ILE DE LA CITE

THE PALAIS DE JUSTICE ON ILE DE LA CITE

THE ARSENAL QUARTER

page 44-45
THE MADELEINE QUARTER
In the 18th century, broad boulevards gradually replaced Charles V's ancient fortified wall stretching from the Madeleine church to Bastille via the Bourse and the Beaubourg quarter. With time, the boulevard des Italiens, boulevard des Capucines and boulevard de la Madeleine evolved into thoroughfares which were most frequently travelled by fashionable Parisians. The triangle formed by the Madeleine, the Opéra and Palais-Royal is still a hub of luxury.

page 46-47
THE PALAIS-ROYAL QUARTER
Cardinal Richelieu commissioned the Palais-Royal, and the Duke of Orléans adorned the gardens with exceptionally elegant galleries and dwellings. It was one of the busiest areas in Paris at the time for courting. It is less lively today in comparison to the surrounding streets, despite the famous columns by Daniel Buren at Palais-Royal. This enchanting spot is ringed by the Bibliothèque Nationale, the Banque de France, the Conseil d'État and the Comédie-Française theatre.

page 52-53
THE MARAIS
The Marais was the quarter of the aristocracy during the 17th century, although the Faubourg Saint-Germain would later usurp this privileged status. In the beginning of the 18th century, the sumptuous mansions of the Marais were broken down and converted into smaller dwellings, often to the detriment of their integrity. Large-scale efforts to restore the area's original glamour have been underway for the past thirty years. It is a hub for culture, art and... nightlife, but, unfortunately a great number living there have had to flee the steep rents.

page 54-55
PLACE DE LA CONCORDE
The Place de la Concorde was initially designed by Jacques-Ange Gabriel to glorify Louis XV. The palaces with Corinthian columns which make up the Crillon hotel and the Ministry of the Marine date from this period. The horses of Marly statues by Guillaume Coustou were added in 1795. In 1835, during Louis-Philippe's reign, the architect Hittorff put on the finishing touches with the famous Luxor obelisk, the fountains and the eight statues representing the main cities of France.

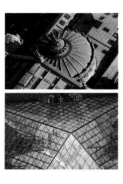

page 60-61
THE OPÉRA
The National Academy of Music and Dance, commissioned by Baron Haussmann, reflects the baroque, eclectic and overwrought Napoléon III style. Built by Charles Garnier, the Opéra was inaugurated during the Third Republic in 1875. The theatre is one of the world's largest in terms of size; and the amount of space devoted to high-society and bourgeois ceremonies was proportionate to the amount of money that was sunk into these affairs.

page 62
THE DOME OF THE OPÉRA

THE GLASS ROOF OF THE PYRAMID
It's as if the monuments of Paris were designed to be seen from the sky, and offer a wide variety of geometric shapes – from the dome of the Opéra to the glass roof of the Pyramid at the Louvre.

page 63
THE BUREN COLUMNS
AT PALAIS-ROYAL

THE MERRY-GO-ROUND
IN THE TUILERIES
The Daniel Buren columns, which have adorned the Court of Honour at Palais-Royal since 1986, draw as many children as the Tuileries Gardens and its attractions do. The columns are as much a treat for the eyes as for the legs.

page 48-49
FORUM DES HALLES
Victor Baltard's elegant metal framework has been replaced by galleries set in glass arcades located in the heart of this very old section of Paris. The square which surrounds the Fountain of the Innocents, the majestic Gothic church of Saint-Eustache and the former wheat market where the Commercial

Exchange now stands are the main landmarks near the Forum des Halles shopping centre. The shopping centre itself is located underground, yet it is still well-lit. People come here to stroll about, as cars have been banned. And it has become a meeting point – especially for young punks.

page 50-51
THE BEAUBOURG QUARTER
The area formed by the Forum des Halles and the Georges Pompidou Centre with its Plateau Beaubourg, a large square sloping down toward the main entrance, is one of great commercial activity. It's a crossroads where all kinds meet, whatever the fashions and however extravagant they

may be. People saunter about, strolling down tiny pedestrian streets, windowshopping in trendy boutiques and art galleries, and finally winding up at an outdoor cafe, overwhelmed. Somehow the beauty of the 17th- and 18th-century buildings get a little lost in the buzz of excitement ...

page 56
THE OBELISK AT LA CONCORDE
This massive monolith of rose syenite, which is over 75 feet high and engraved with hieroglyphics lauding the great deeds of Ramses II, comes from the pharoah's temple in Thebes. The obelisk, which dates from the 13th century B.C., was given to Louis-Philippe by Mehemet-Ali in 1831.

page 57-58
PLACE VENDÔME
Like all the royal squares, the Place Vendôme lost the statue of its creator during the Revolution. Louis XIV stepped aside to make room for the Austerlitz column. Moulded of bronze from the cannons captured from the Russians and Austrians, the column is topped by a statue of

Emperor Napoléon. This lovely square was built in the 17th century by Jules Hardouin-Mansart, and, with its posh jewellery boutiques and the Ritz hotel, is the gem case of Paris.

page 59
THE OPÉRA AND SURROUNDING AREA
Baron Haussmann razed, gutted, levelled and destroyed anything which obstructed his vision of laying out broad boulevards linking important squares. To do this, he broke through streets and vital centres, such as the Opéra and its surrounding area.

page 64-65
THE LOUVRE
The original fortress of the Louvre was built during Philippe-Auguste's reign, in 1190, and was then expanded under Charles V during the 14th century. From Francois Ier on, each generation left its mark. The 20th century was not going to be left out: a glass pyramid, designed by I.M. Pei, was erected in the main courtyard. Its four glistening sides reflect the sky, as well as the classic facades of the palace. In addition, the Louvre is well on

its way to becoming the world's largest museum: the Finance Ministry recently moved out of a wing, thus freeing up space for new galleries.

page 66-67
THE SAINT-GERMAIN-L'AUXERROIS CHURCH
Saint-Germain-l'Auxerrois, the church of the Louvre and parish for the French royal family, is a key Gothic monument, despite several changes it has undergone over the centuries. Although it is boxed into an arena of imposing architecture (the 17th-century colonnade of the Louvre's eastern facade, the 19th-century municipality of the first arrondissement, and the department store buildings like La Samaritaine, which

date from the beginning of this century), the church has preserved its slender, graceful silhouette.

FORUM DES HALLES AND SURROUNDING AREA

THE MARAIS

ONE OF THE HORSES OF MARLY ON PLACE DE LA CONCORDE

THE OBELISK ON PLACE DE LA CONCORDE

THE OPERA AND SURROUNDING AREA

THE DOME OF THE OPERA THE GLASS ROOF OF THE PYRAMID

THE BUREN COLUMNS AT PALAIS-ROYAL   THE MERRY-GO-ROUND AT THE TUILERIES   63

THE LOUVRE

THE SAINT-GERMAIN-L'AUXERRO'S CHURCH

page 70-71
THE COMMERCIAL EXCHANGE
AT THE FORUM DES HALLES
All that remains of the magnificent mansion that the architect Bullant built here in 1572 for Catherine de Médicis, the Hôtel de Soissons, is a 100-foot-high fluted column. The column was said to have been used by Catherine de Médicis' astrologist, Ruggieri, as an observatory deck for stargazing. The old wheat market commissioned in 1765-1768 by the provost of the merchants, de Viarmes, was covered with a metal dome in 1811. The Doric columns which adorn the half-moon square of the rue de Viarmes are in total harmony with the Commercial Exchange which stands there today.

page 72-73
THE GEORGES POMPIDOU CENTRE
The avant-garde architecture and scintillating colours of the Georges Pompidou Centre, better known as Beaubourg, really stand out in this old quarter of Paris. Musicians, magicians, fire-swallowers and other travelling showmen who perform on the parvis of the Georges Pompidou square preserve the traditional feel of the "Beau Bourg", or beautiful burg, area. These days, there are more tourists who visit the Pompidou Centre than the Eiffel Tower!

page 78-79
THE BASTILLE AREA
Victor Hugo described the Colonne de Juillet as "a monument manqué for an aborted Revolution". Topped by the Spirit of Liberty, the column was erected in 1833 to commemorate the victims of the July 1830 revolution. One hundred fifty-four feet high, it rules over this large crossroads of old Paris between the noble Marais and the turbulent faubourg. The new Bastille opera sits like a large beached ship, looking somewhat incongruous.

page 80
LA SAMARITAINE DEPARTMENT STORE

THE SAINT-EUSTACHE CHURCH
The transparency of the green glass casings of the Samaritaine store meets the finesse of the apse of the Saint-Germain-l'Auxerrois church – similar to the way that the Forum des Halles arcades meet the Saint-Eustache church.

page 81
THE BASTILLE OPERA
Commissioned by President François Mitterrand, the "opera of the people" at Bastille, was designed by the architect Carlos Ott.

PLACE DES VICTOIRES
The work of one of Louis XIV's great courtisans, Marshal de la Feuillade, the Place des Victoires was designed in 1685 by Hardouin-Mansart.

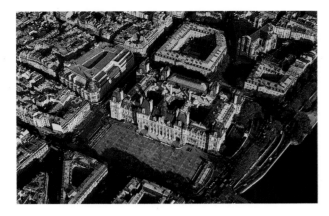

page 74-75
HÔTEL DE VILLE (CITY HALL)
After the city hall built by François Ier's
Italian architect, Domenico, called Le
Boccador, was burnt down during the
Commune, architects Théodore Ballu and
Édouard Deperthes rebuilt a similar edifice
in 1882. The luminous city hall, with its
whitewashed exterior, is situated between
the old Place de Grève which is now
reserved for pedestrians, and the parvis of
the Saint-Gervais-Saint-Protais church.
The sparkling fountains which surround it
are by F.X. Lalanne.

page 76-77
PLACE DES VOSGES
In 1612, the tournament of the knights of
glory was held to celebrate the engagement
of Louis XIII and Anne of Austria. This
ceremony marked the inauguration of the
Place Royale, even though its creator –
Henri IV – had died two years earlier. This
square, which was rebaptised Place des
Vosges in 1800, was home to many famous
people – Sully, Bossuet, Alphonse Daudet
and Victor Hugo. The thirty-six brick and
stone pavilions that line the arcades are exceptionally elegant.

page 82-83
THE GEORGES POMPIDOU CENTRE
In 1969, President Georges Pompidou de-
cided to erect a centre for art and culture
on the Plateau Beaubourg. He entrusted
the architects R. Rogers and Renzo Piano
with the project, and they designed a hive-
like structure atop a steel skeleton. People
are intrigued by the huge brightly co-
loured metal pipes and a double escalator
which snakes up the side of the building.
The building was designed from the
inside, in order to maximise space for
exhibits and for work.

page 84-85
HÔTEL DE VILLE
The facade of the city hall was designed
with niches, footing and columns for the
statues of the allegories and the one hundred and eight famous Parisians. The statues of thirty French cities stand above the
entablature crowning the building. The
pediment of the clock in the centre of the
building features some beautiful statues:
the Seine and the Marne by Aine Millet;
Education and Work by Ernest Miolle;
and, higher up, the allegory representing
the city of Paris by Jean Gauthien.

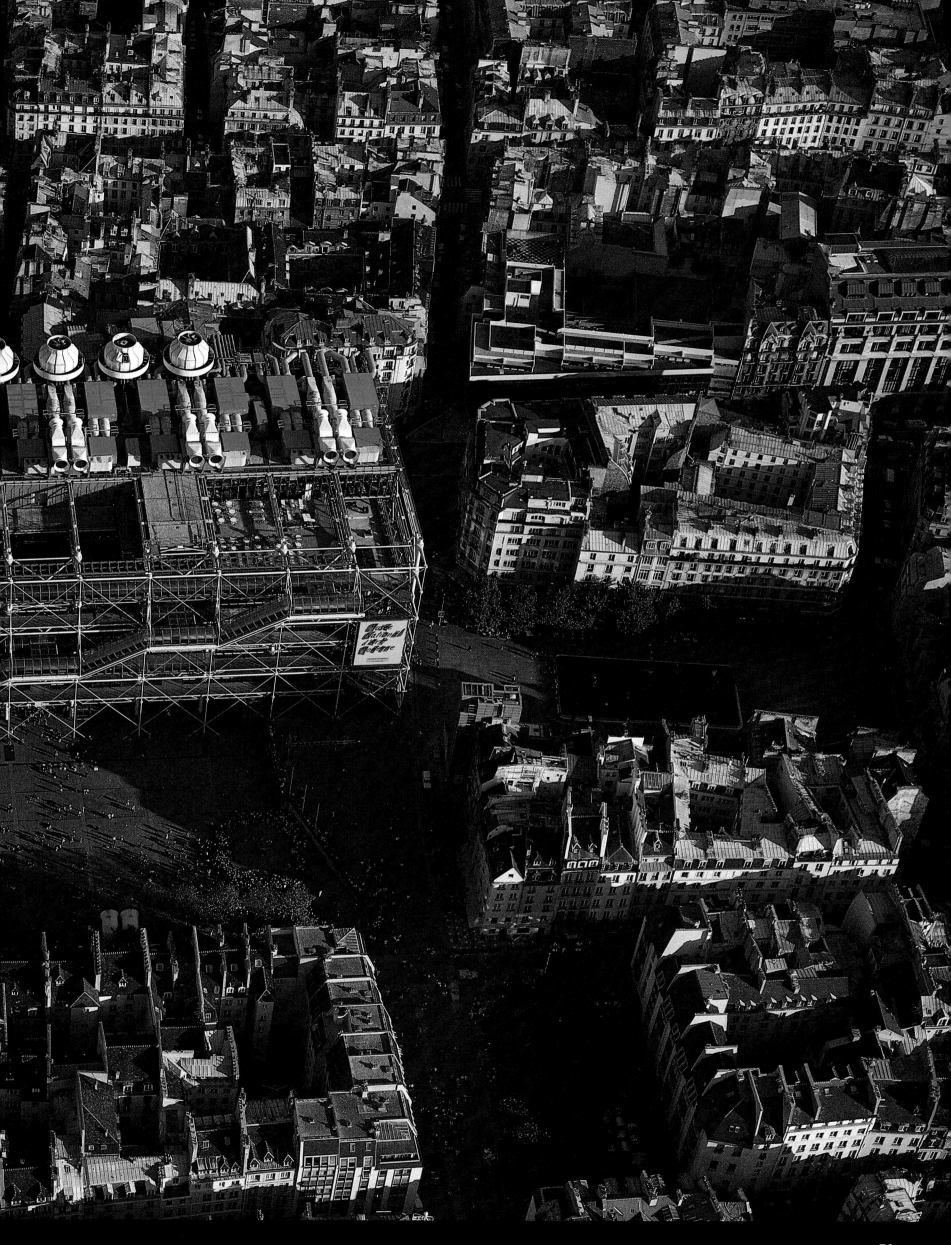

LA SAMARITAINE DEPARTMENT STORE

THE SAINT-EUSTACHE CHURCH

PLACE DES VICTOIRES

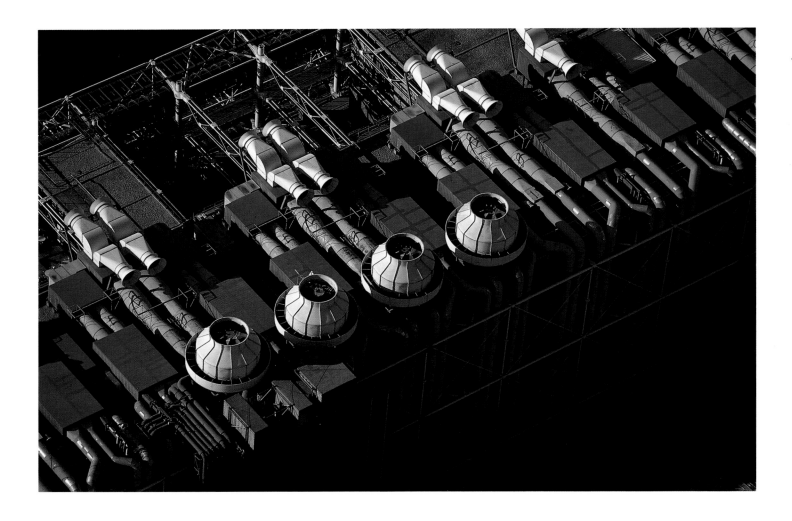

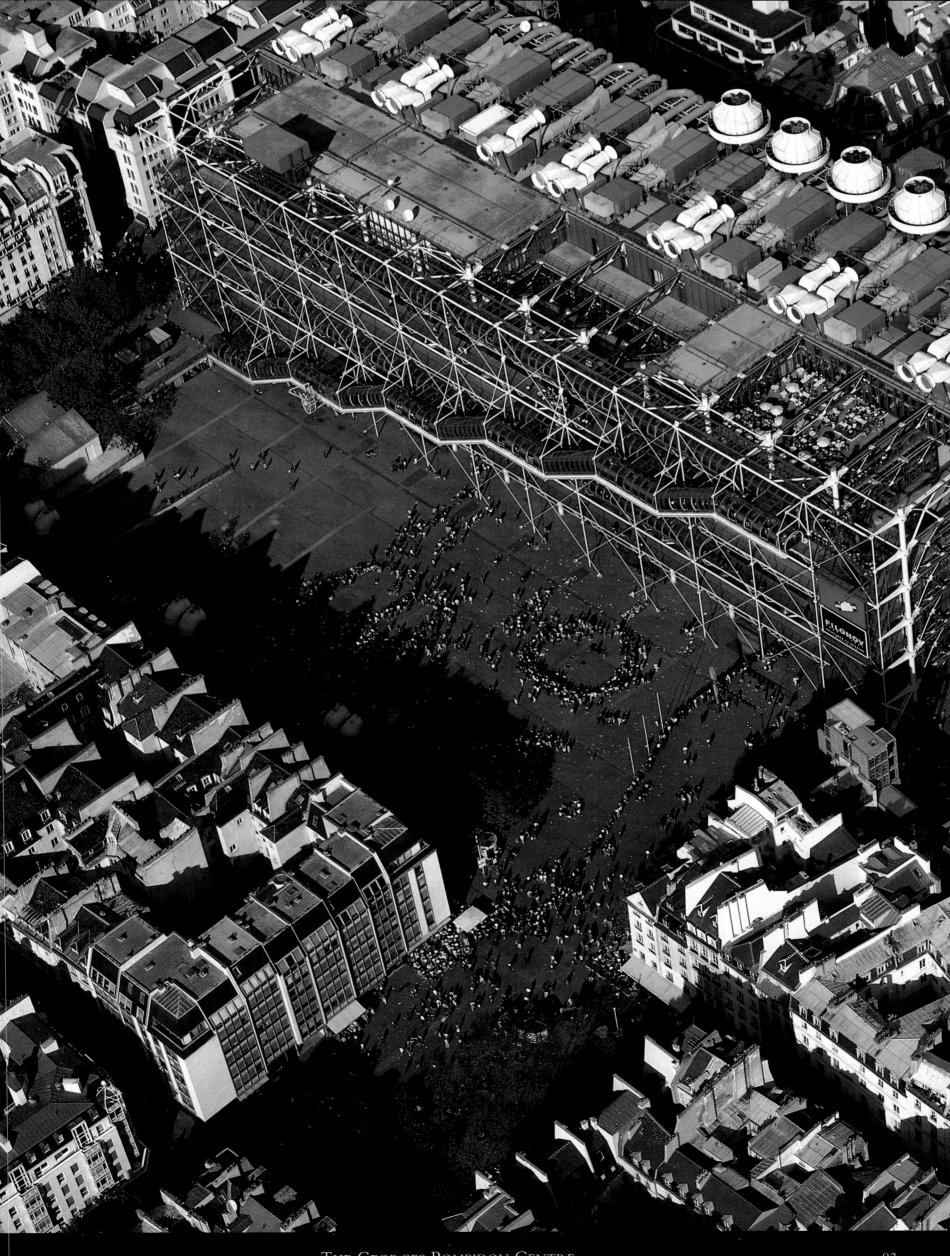

Hotel de Ville

page 88

THE PARC DES PRINCES STADIUM

The Parc des Princes, inaugurated in 1972, was designed by the architect Roger Taillibert. This covered stadium was one of the first to be built without using posts, thus ensuring perfect visibility for each of the fifty thousand seats.

page 89

PALAIS DES CONGRÈS
AT PORTE MAILLOT

Built by the architects Gillet, Maloletenkov and Guiboud, the Palais des Congrès and the International Centre of Paris are a hub of activity in the city's western regions for ballets, concerts, films and shopping.

page 90-91

PORTE MAILLOT

Porte Maillot is one of the busiest areas in western Paris. Located at the junction of the beltways and the area stretching from Étoile to La Défense, the Palais des Congrès offers suburban-dwellers the possibility of finding entertainment without having to face the bottlenecks of Paris. It is a miniature city in itself, with nineteen conference rooms, three exposition halls, an auditorium, a hotel, four cinemas, restaurants and various boutiques.

page 96-97

PARC MONCEAU

Louis-Philippe commissioned Carmontelle, known for his work in the theatre and as a brilliant sketcher, to dream up "an Anglo-Chinese garden" in the midst of the Monceau Plain, which was abundant in game. The Revolution came and went, then Haussmann began work on rebuilding the city. He designed boulevard Malesherbes to cut right through the park! Pereire purchased the eastern sector and turned it into one of Paris' most luxurious neighbourhoods. Haussmann had Alphand redesign the other half and surrounded it with a belt of beautiful hotels.

page 98-99

GARE SAINT-LAZARE
AND PLACE DE L'EUROPE

The first railway, which stretched from Pecq to Paris, was built in 1836. The terminus at Gare Saint-Lazare was completed in 1843, but the station which stands today wasn't begun until 1885, by the architect Juste Lisch, and completed in 1889. Waves of journeymen used to pour out of the station each day towards the great metropolis; they've since been replaced by thousands of suburban commuters. The Place de l'Europe looks almost as if it were suspended above the groups of sidings.

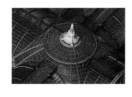

page 104-105

THE CHAMPS-ÉLYSÉES GARDENS

Many pavilions stand in the Champs-Élysées Gardens which Hittorff laid out in 1838: Élysée-Lenôtre, Gabriel-Potel et Chabot, the Ledoyen restaurant and the Espace Cardin. But there is also the Marigny theatre, the Rond-Point theatre (formerly the Palais des Glaces), and the Petit Palais and Grand Palais. The two theatres were built at approximately the same period, towards the end of the 19th century, and were the first to experiment with panorama. Their domes are in harmony with the Rond-Point of the Champs-Élysées.

page 106-107

THE GRAND PALAIS

Girault oversaw the building of the Grand Palais, which was to be "the Republic's monument to the glory of French art". Récipon's flying quadriga erected over the corner staircases are proof enough of this! The great iron hall, capped by Daydé and Pillé's dome, gives a strikingly light touch to the palace and its academic stone facades.

page 92-93
THE GOLDEN TRIANGLE
IN THE SIXTEENTH DISTRICT
This is one of Paris's most elegant quarters located in the area around Étoile, the Place Victor-Hugo and Porte Dauphine. Many famous people have lived here, like the writers Victor Hugo, Anatole France and Paul Valéry; artists Kees Van Dongen, Berthe Morisot and Eugène Manet; and musicians like Debussy. The boutiques and restaurants here are as elegant as the town houses and opulent buildings. The water reservoirs seem a little out of place in this classical setting.

page 94
AVENUE FOCH
AND THE DAUPHINE QUARTER
Avenue Foch came about as a result of Haussmann's transformation of the Bois de Boulogne. The architect Hittorff stretched this imperial thoroughfare from the Porte Dauphine (J. Carlu's Université Dauphine) to Étoile.

page 95
PLACE CHARLES-DE-GAULLE
BETTER KNOWN AS ÉTOILE
The avenue de la Grande Armée and the Champs-Élysées are two arteries which penetrate the heart of Paris with a single arrow. Place de l'Étoile, which Napoléon ringed with twelve hotels by Hittorff, features Alphand's tree-filled gardens, which breathe air into this turntable of congested traffic.

page 100-101
THE SAINT-AUGUSTIN CHURCH
The Saint-Augustin church, a mix of imitated styles, is located at the junction of the broad tumultuous boulevard Malesherbes and boulevard Haussmann. Looking somewhat forlorn, the church was built between 1860 and 1871 to fill a vacuum. It was constructed onto a metal frame, the work of the architect Victor Baltard. The church pales in comparison to the chic bourgeois buildings dating from Napoléon III's time which surround it; only the Renaissance-inspired dome matches the grandeur.

page 102-103
THE ÉLYSÉE PALACE
Between the avenue Gabriel and the rue du Faubourg Saint-Honoré stands the mansion where the French presidents have lived since 1873. Inside the walls lies a lovely English park. The Élysée Palace was built in 1718 by Mollet for the Count of Evreux, expanded by Alexandre Hardouin, and raised under Napoléon III. Madame de Pompadour, the Murats, Joséphine, Napoléon, Alexander the Tsar and, temporarily, Louis-Napoléon Bonaparte have all lived here.

page 108-109
THE PETIT PALAIS
AND THE GRAND PALAIS
The Petit and Grand Palais run along the Cours-la-Reine promenade, which is lined with the chestnut trees planted by Marie de Médicis. Built for the 1900 World Exhibition, they house art collections, exhibits, Salons, and even entire museums, such as the Palais de la Découverte. The Alexandre III bridge, which leads to the Invalides esplanade, reveals the same degree of technical audacity and luxuriance as the Art Nouveau palaces.

THE PARC DES PRINCES STADIUM

THE PALAIS DES CONGRES AT PORTE MAILLOT

Porte Maillot

PLACE CHARLES DE GAULLE, BETTER KNOWN AS ETOILE

THE ROND-POINT THEATRE IN THE CHAMPS-ELYSEES GARDENS

THE MARIGNY THEATRE

page 112-113
PLACE DU TERTRE IN MONTMARTRE
In comparison to the other outlying villages which the decree of 1860 moved inside the district of Paris, Montmartre has best preserved its picturesque character. Rimmed with beautiful little houses often hidden by the hordes of tourists, the Place du Tertre has been invaded by restaurants and cafés. The square may be peppered with painters' easels, but it's a far cry from the true artistic tradition of the quarter.

page 114-115
THE SACRÉ-CŒUR BASILICA IN MONTMARTRE
The Sacré-Cœur basilica stands high above the rest of Paris, a bright white beacon. With its neo-Romano-Byzantine style, it stands out rather strangely against the charming little houses of the quarter. Plans were drawn up for the basilica by Abadie in 1876; it was built by Daumet, Laisné, Rauline and Magne in 1910. Until the Revolution, there was a Benedictine monastery on the hill near the Sacré-Cœur. There was a chapel as well, which the basilica loomed over in a slightly odd way.

page 120-121
THE CANAL SAINT-MARTIN QUARTER
The Canal Saint-Martin, inaugurated in 1825, is an extension of the Ourcq canal. From the La Villette basin to the Arsenal basin, it travels nearly three miles across nine locks. The Granges-aux-belles area, located in front of the Place du colonel-Fabien near the Communist Party headquarters (built in 1968-1971 by Neimeyer), forms a totally independent little quarter. The nearby buildings of the Saint-Louis hospital form a little village.

page 122-123
PARC DES BUTTES-CHAUMONT
Like Montmartre, the *butte*, or hill, at Chaumont was well-known for its sand quarries. What a feat to have transformed this rugged area of ill-repute into such a strangely baroque fairytale landscape! A team of artists for Napoléon III were responsible for this metamorphosis – Alphand, Barillet, Davioud, and the Prince Puckler-Muskau all worked on the quarter and the lovely Buttes-Chaumont park.

page 128
THE GRANDS MOULINS DE PANTIN

THE MAGASINS GÉNÉRAUX ALONG THE LA VILLETTE BASIN
Both the Grands Moulins de Pantin and the Magasins Généraux (General Stores) remain intact (except for one of the latter's buildings having burnt down recently). These 19th-century warehouses, which almost seem to float, have been converted into artists' ateliers, and close the perspective of the La Villette basin.

page 129
SMALL SUBURBAN-LIKE PAVILIONS NEAR PLACE RHIN ET DANUBE
Who would ever imagine that suburban-like areas where the masses live are still lurking inside Paris? In tiny, perfectly parallel streets between Pré-Saint-Gervais and the Buttes-Chaumont park, little narrow pavilions are lined up neatly like trees in a row.

page 130-131
THE CREMATORIUM AT PÈRE-LACHAISE CEMETERY
In 1801, the prefect Frochot signed a decree which imposed stringent public sanitation rules. A decision was made to create three cemeteries outside Paris: the cimetière du Nord, Montmartre, in the north; cimetière du Sud, Montparnasse, in the south; and Père-Lachaise in the east. Located on the slope of a hill, Père-Lachaise was laid out like a park by Brongniart. Few know about the Columbarium, with the crematorium in its centre, which Formigé built at the end of the 19th century.

page 116-117

GARE DU NORD
AND GARE DE L'EST

The Paris train stations and French railway system dates from Napoléon III. The highly elegant Gare du Nord, built by Hittorff, and Dusquesney's Gare de l'Est were laid out side by side in the tenth arrondissement. The wide boulevard Magenta and the rue La Fayette cut through this quarter, which was rebuilt by Haussmann. Numerous hospitals, such as Lariboisière, Fernand-Widal and Saint-Lazare were created at the time as well.

page 118-119

PLACE DE LA RÉPUBLIQUE

The Place de la République was built in several instalments, growing little by little as more boulevards came into existence.. In 1883, it was named after the bronze statue built by the Morice brothers which stands in the centre. Two large buildings frame the rue du Faubourg du Temple on the northeastern side of the square. They are the former Magasins Réunis, founded in 1866 (what is today the Printemps department store) and the Vérines barracks, built in 1854.

page 124

A GROUP OF BUILDINGS
ON RUE MARCADET

PLACE STALINGRAD

Flying over the city can reveal geometric forms unknown to the passer-by, like this group of buildings located on the rue Marcadet or the inside of a rotunda at La Villette that was built by Ledoux in 1784.

page 125

THE GREEK TEMPLE
IN THE PARC DES BUTTES-CHAUMONT

The architects who created the Buttes-Chaumont park transformed this rugged terrain into a landscape of ruins and rocks. A rock mass in the middle of the lake forms an island, where a lovely little Greek temple stands.

page 126-127

PARC DE LA VILLETTE

The architect A. Fainsilber had to utilise the immense carcass of the slaughterhouses on the Ourcq canal, which had gone out of business in 1973, to build a science and industry centre at La Villette. He surrounded the slaughterhouses with water by installing a moat system, and covered the facades with grey granite and blue steel. Chamayon's shiny stainless-steel globe is like a huge mirror for the surroundings. This hemispheric projection room is a mark of technological and artistic success.

page 132-133

THE MARKET ON RUE D'ALIGRE

Located south of the rue du Faubourg Saint-Antoine, the rue d'Aligre comes to life each morning in a burst of colours and sounds. Here is the famous marché d'Aligre, a bustling market which offers second-hand goods and clothes on the square, and fruits and vegetables in the street!

page 134

THE GARE DE LYON CLOCK TOWER

The Gare de Lyon, dominated by its high clock tower, was built by Marius Toudoire in 1899, then expanded in 1927. The 76 million people who travel to and from the Gare de Lyon and Bercy each year can set their watches as soon as they arrive.

page 135

THE BOULEVARD PÉRIPHÉRIQUE
AT PORTE DE BERCY

What an anthill! People may be moving more and more to the suburbs, but the density of the population in Paris remains very high, encroaching upon vital living space. Road and rail traffic cannot keep pace with the booming rhythm of the capital.

Place du Tertre in Montmartre

The Sacre-Cœur Basilica in Montmartre

GARE DU NORD AND GARE DE L'EST

THE CANAL SAINT-MARTIN QUARTER

A GROUP OF BUILDINGS ON RUE MARCADET   PLACE STALINGRAD

THE TEMPLE IN THE PARC DES BUTTES-CHAUMONT

128   THE GRANDS MOULINS DE PANTIN   THE MAGASINS GENERAUX ALONG THE LA VILLETTE BASIN

Small suburban-like pavilions near Place Rhin et Danube

The Crematorium at Pere-Lachaise cemetery

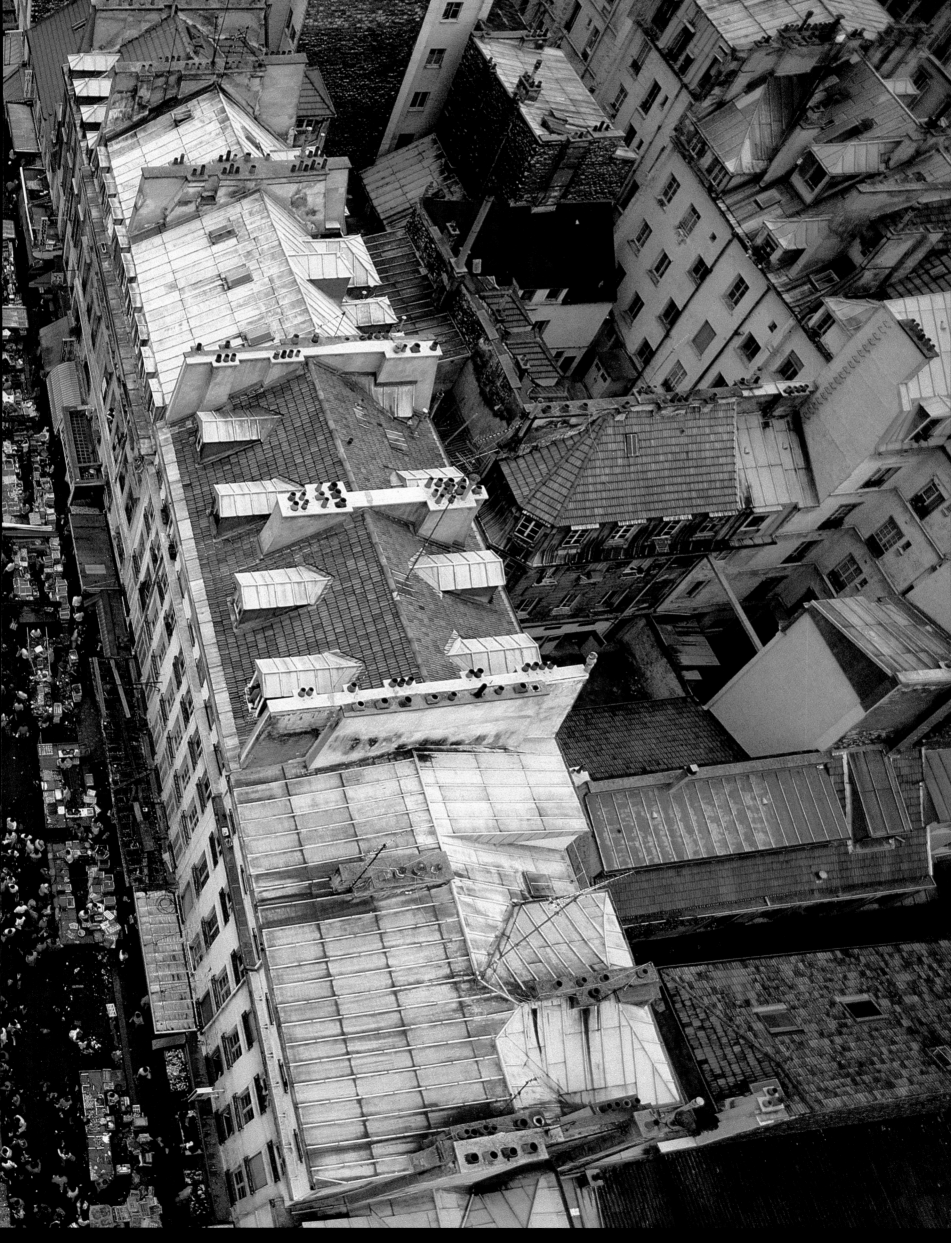

134   THE GARE DE LYON CLOCK TOWER

page 138-139

THE HÔTEL ROYAL AT LES INVALIDES
"Among the diverse establishments which we have built during the course of our reign, none is more useful to the State than the Hôtel Royal at les Invalides." The lines were excerpted from Louis XIV's testament. By bequeathing to Paris a military hospital, he left it one of the most perfect monuments of the classical period. Napoléon I is buried here.

page 140-141

THE INVALIDES DOME
When J. Hardouin Mansart edified the Dome church at les Invalides between 1679 and 1706, he grafted it onto the Saint-Louis-des-Invalides church, called "of the Soldiers", which he had already built according to Libéral Bruant's design. Its resplendent dome was again covered in gold leaf for the celebration of the Bicentennial of the French Revolution in 1989. The Saint-Louis church is the royal entrance, the entrance of honour is off the esplanade.

page 146-147

THE SORBONNE
AND SURROUNDING AREA
The Sorbonne stretches across a large quadrilateral area from the rue des Écoles to the rue de la Sorbonne. Paris IV and Paris III university centres are situated here, as well as the École des Chartes. Richelieu commissioned the architect Le Mercier to build a series of sumptuous buildings, but only the striking chapel with its dome remains. The other buildings were rebuilt by the architect Nénot at the end of the 19th century. To the east, lie the elite Collège de France, the Lycée-Louis-le-Grand (Molière and Voltaire studied here), and the Law School.

page 148-149

THE PANTHÉON QUARTER
The mayoralty of the fifth arrondissement and the Law School, situated up and down the rue Soufflot, form one side of the Place du Panthéon. The former was built by Hittorff in the middle of the 19th century, the latter begun in 1771 by Soufflot but redone dozens of times since. To the north of the square, the Sainte-Geneviève monastic library has stood since 1624, although the buildings which house its heritage date from the middle of the 19th century, built by Labrouste.

page 154-155

THE LUXEMBOURG GARDENS
The royal gardens of Luxembourg became public property under the Second Empire. Relatively few people know that there are tennis-courts near the main fountain. To the south of the Médicis fountain, the École des Mines encroaches on what used to be part of the park. The rue Soufflot, between Marie de Médicis' Luxembourg Gardens and Louis X's Panthéon, is crammed with students milling about. They head for the park to study for exams on the shady lawns.

page 156-157

THE MAINE-MONTPARNASSE QUARTER
The Montparnasse Tower, the highest in Europe, looks out over the Montparnasse railway station. A major urban development plan by the architects Lopez, Baudouin, Arretche, du Hoym and Dubuisson covered the railway tracks between the Vaugirard and Plaisance build-ings with a large stone slab where a garden and buildings stand. The architect Ricardo Bofill designed a a group of neo-classical buildings around the Place de Catalogne, Place de l'Amphithéâtre and Place des Colonnes, complete with pediments, pilasters, columns and entablatures.

page 142
THE SAINT-SULPICE CHURCH
Saint-Sulpice is one of the largest churches in Paris, and one of the richest. Its construction spans the 17th and 18th centuries. The two main architects were Gittard and Servandoni.

page 143
INSTITUT DE FRANCE
Cardinal Mazarin provided for the construction of the Collège des Quatre Nations, or college of four nations, which became the Institut de France under Napoléon. This masterpiece by Le Vau, with its famous dome, comprises five academies.

page 144-145
THE SAINT-GERMAIN-DES-PRÉS QUARTER
The area around Saint-Sulpice specialised in religious art, but the main centre of activity at Saint-Germain-des-Prés shifted north to the rue Bonaparte. Art galleries and antique shops around the École des Beaux-Arts, or fine arts institute, followed the specialised editors and book shops in their trek north. The world of fashion came onto the scene as well. People come here to stroll about, but there's plenty to buy too.

page 150-151
THE PANTHÉON
In the 12th century, the Sainte-Geneviève abbey dominated the entire top of the Sainte-Geneviève hill. Only the bell-tower, called "the Tower of Clovis", remains today, and has been incorporated into the Lycée Henri IV. The Saint-Etienne-du-Mont church was built during the Renaissance, and in the 18th century, the Panthéon was erected over the ruins of the abbey. The Panthéon is now a church with frescoes by Puvis de Chavannes and a crypt, which holds the remains of Voltaire, Zola and Jean Moulin.

page 152-153
THE LUXEMBOURG PALACE
Marie de Médicis purchased the Hôtel de Luxembourg and its surrounding area; then commissioned Salomon de Brosse to build a palace which would remind her of the Pitti Palace in Florence, where she spent her childhood. In 1795, it was the seat of the Directoire under Napoléon; in 1800, the seat of the Senate. The lower house, the Chamber of Peers, occupied the quarters during the Restoration, but in 1858, it resumed its earlier status as seat of the Senate, thanks to Louis-Philippe.

page 158-159
THE OBSERVATORY
Built at the end of the 17th century, this beautiful edifice is the world's oldest observatory in use today. It was constructed according to Claude Perrault's design, but the angle of the buildings had been predetermined by a group of mathematicians from the Royal Academy of Sciences to respect the Meridian of Paris. The observatory, which has been affiliated with the Meudon observatory since 1926 and with the radioastronomy station at Nançay since the Fifties, has become one of the world's top research centres for astronomy.

THE SAINT-SULPICE CHURCH

INSTITUT DE FRANCE

THE SAINT-GERMAIN-DES-PRES QUARTER

THE SORBONNE AND SURROUNDING AREA

THE PANTHEON QUARTER

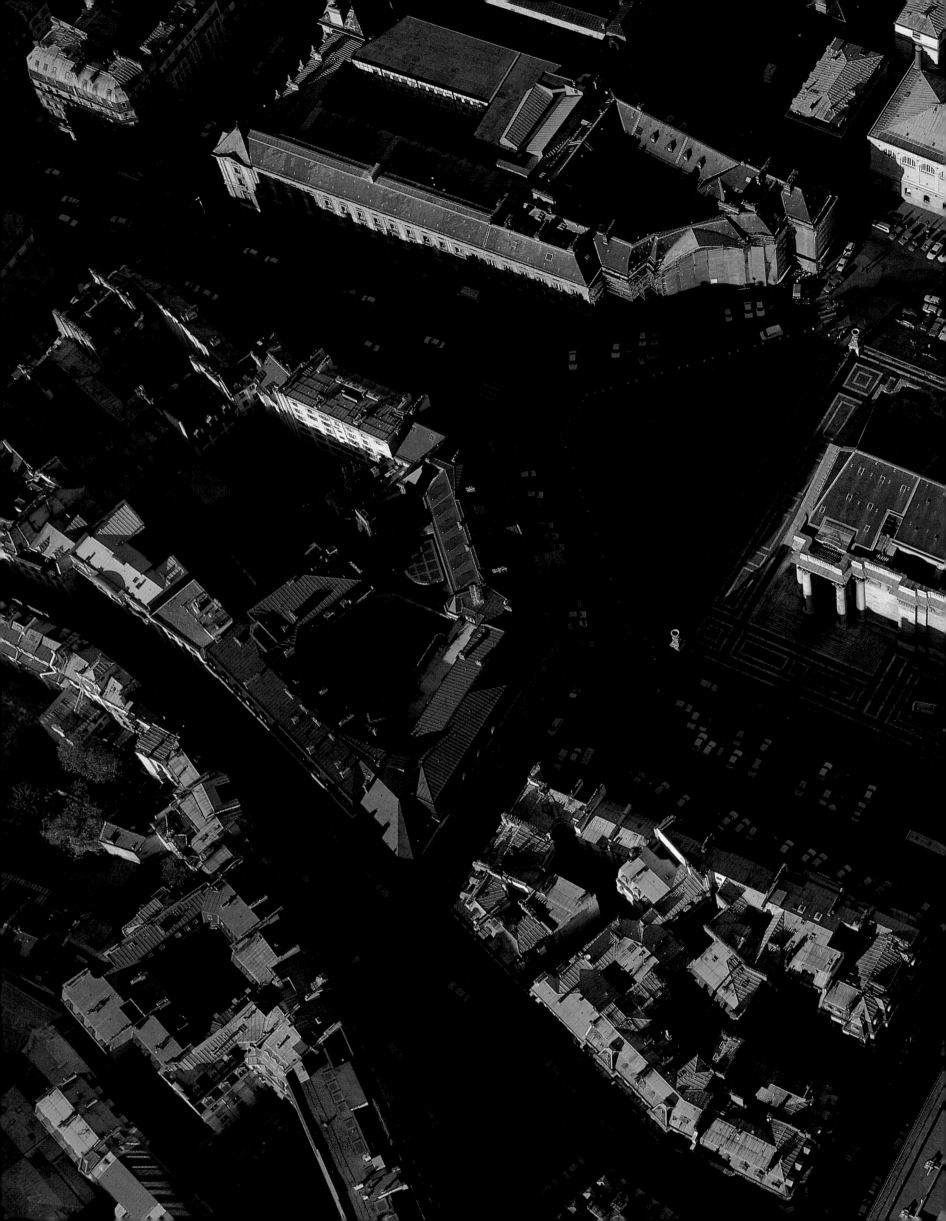

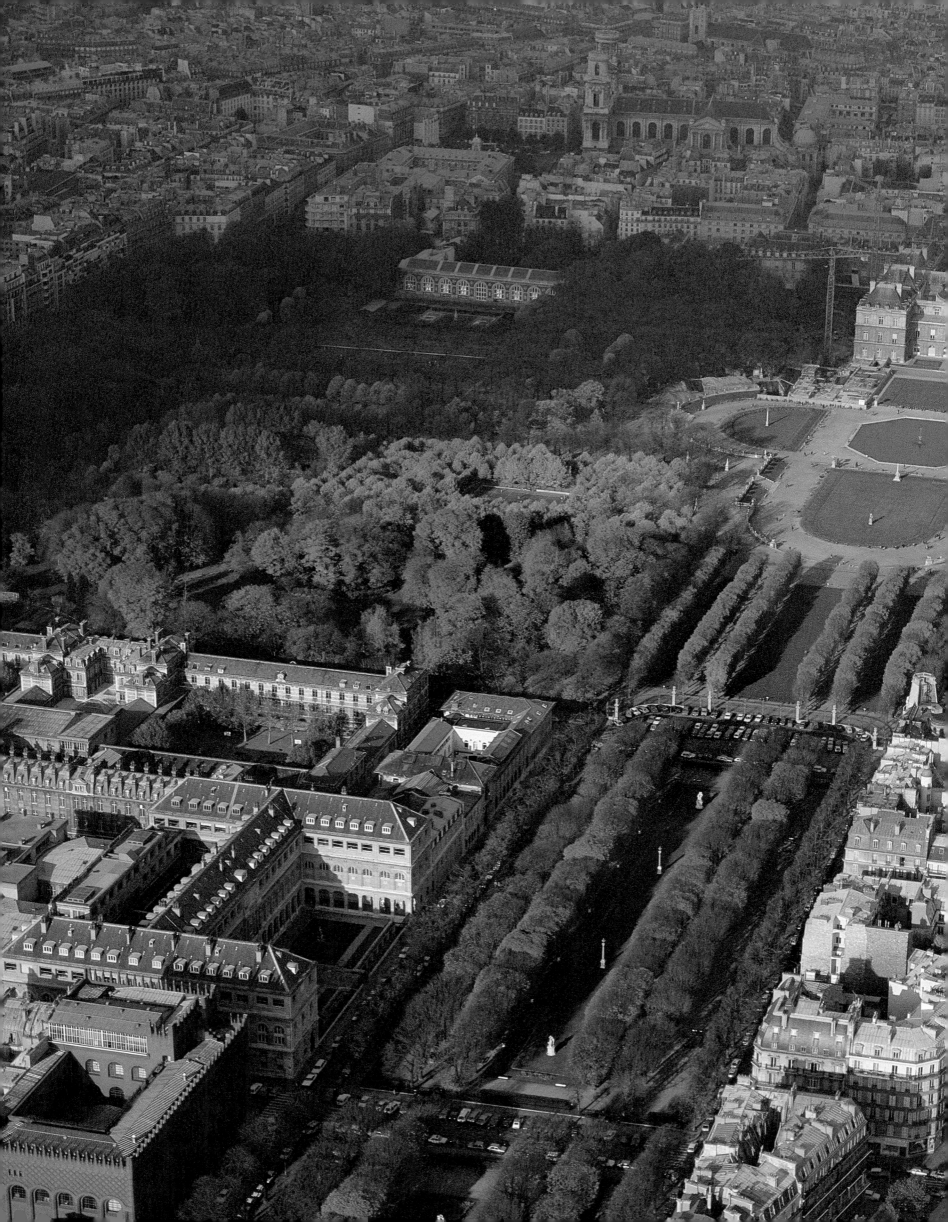

page 161
JARDIN DES PLANTES
The 19th-century buildings at one end of the Jardin des Plantes house scientists from the Natural History Museum, but the garden itself dates from the 17th century. There is a great variety of animals in the menagerie.

page 162-163
A HIGH-RISE AT PORTE D'ITALIE
The Place d'Italie is surrounded by large building complexes and high-rises which bear the name of Italian cities. This is the main exit from southwest Paris, but the people who live in the high-rises don't really need to leave for the country or stretch out in the lovely Hélène-Boucher

or Robert-Bajac Squares to enjoy the sunshine. Their panoramic terraces are totally private and sheltered from intrusive eyes!

page 164-165
THE SALPÊTRIÈRE HOSPITAL
Louis XIV converted Louis XIII's Grand Arsenal into a "general hospital for the poor", as well as a prison for women. It was turned into an asylum in 1796. Le Vau and Le Muet were the architects who worked on the hospital, but history has relegated them to the shadows in comparison to Libéral Bruant, who built the Saint-Louis chapel between 1657 and 1677. Shaped like a Greek cross, the chapel seems in a totally different vein than the other more classical buildings.

page 166
ROLAND-GARROS
More and more tennis fans keep coming to the stadium at Roland-Garros each June. Due to popular demand – both commercially and socially, the City of Paris will surely grant it more territory on which to expand.

page 167
THE HIGH-RISE GARDENS
AT PORTE DE LA MUETTE
The well-heeled set is always on the stake-out for greenery, whether in the suburbs immediately west of Paris or at la Muette. The terraces of this building complex, located just off the Bois de Boulogne, were surely planted and tended by die-hard ecologists...

page 168-169
THE FOIRE DU TRÔNE
AMUSEMENT PARK
As soon as the weather warms up, members of a travelling show set up shop in a huge area located on the edge of the woods at bois de Vincennes, where Parisians come for fun and games. Whether it's the scary Toboggan to Hell roller-coaster for speed freaks, or the humble ferris wheel, this huge amusement park provides fun for all ages in a country-fair atmosphere.

page 170-173
THE ARCHE AT LA DÉFENSE
Erected in the heart of Paris's newest business quarter, the Arche de la Défense represents a brief respite from the look of modernity, elegance and utility of the area. Designed by the architect Otto von Spreckelsen and inaugurated during festivities for the 1989 Bicentennial for the French Revolution, the glass and Carrara marble structure elegantly punctuates the vista stretching to the Pyramid at the Louvre. The International Foundation for Human Rights is located in its rooftop offices.

A HIGH-RISE AT PORTE D'ITALIE

THE SALPÊTRIÈRE HOSPITAL

THE HIGH-RISE GARDENS AT PORTE DE LA MUETTE

THE FOIRE DU TRONE ON THE EDGE OF THE BOIS DE VINCENNES

The Grande Arche at La Defense

TABLE OF CONTENTS

INDEX

Jean-Marie Chourgnoz

ACKNOWLEDGEMENTS

I should like to extend my heartfelt thanks
to the President of the Republic, Francois Mitterrand,
to Mr. Francois de Grossouvre,
and to the Prefect of the Paris Police for his help.

The photographs were taken from a twin-engine Ecureuil
from the company Heli-France at the Issy-les-Moulineaux heliport.
(Tel: 1 – 45.57.53.67)
I would particularly like to thank Joel Bastien and his pilots,
Bernard Fournier and Richard Sarrazy,
and Mr. Cotinaud from Aerospatiale.

I also would like to thank the photographers, who are also my friends,
who helped me during this air-borne project,
Philippe Bourseiller and Nicolas Tavernier,
as well as my assistant, Frank Lechenet.

The photographs were shot on Kodachrome 64 ASA film
and on Ektachrome 64 and 100 ASA,
and were developed by Rush Labo in Paris.

Certain photographs in this book were taken from a nacelle
from the company LEV. Thanks in particular to Gilles Desouza.

Photographs distributed by ALTITUDES
30, rue des Favorites – 75015 Paris

Photogravure by Raballand

Printed in Switzerland by Weber Press in Bienne
Dépôt légal n° 6013 – juillet 1996
I.S.B.N. 2.85108.820.3
34/0982/8